Wild America

j. lockhart

Wild America

Portrayed by JAMES LOCKHART

Publishers since 1798

THOMAS NELSON INC., *Publishers*

Nashville / New York

PUBLISHER'S NOTE

It has been the desire of the publisher to make *Wild America* one of the finest examples of the bookmaking art to have appeared in recent decades. This effort required the cooperation of a great many people. The publisher and the artist wish to recognize the following firms and to cite the particular services which they rendered.

The type face selected for this book is primarily Melior, Roman and Italic, which was designed in 1948–1949 by Hermann Zapf as a specially legible type face for Linotype. The actual setting for this book was done by The Clarinda Company, Clarinda, Iowa, and by April Graphics Studio, Northfield, Illinois.

Wild America was printed by offset lithography by Sleepeck Printing Company, Bellwood, Illinois, which also made most of the four–color separations. Special fade–resistant inks were used. So that the artist would be certain that the color reproductions would be as much like the original paintings as possible, Mr. Lockhart worked directly with the color etchers, camera technicians, plate makers, and even the men who operated the four–color presses.

The paper stock for this book was carefully chosen and manufactured to the artist's specifications. The heavy embossed print paper and the text paper were manufactured by the Potlatch Corporation, Northwest Paper Division, of Cloquet, Minnesota, and supplied by Bradner–Smith & Company, Chicago, Illinois.

The binding material used on this book is Special Record Buckram provided by the Holliston Mills, Inc., Kingsport, Tennessee, and the binding was done by Nicholstone Book Bindery, Inc., Nashville, Tennessee.

Nature doth thus kindly heal every wound. By the mediation of a thousand little mosses and fungi, the most unsightly objects become radiant of beauty. There seem to be two sides of this world, presented us at different times, as we see things in gross or dissolution, in life or death. For seen with the eye of the poet, as God sees them, all things are alive and beautiful; but seen with the historical eye, or eye of memory, they are dead and offensive. If we see Nature as pausing, immediately all mortifies and decays; but seen as progressing, she is beautiful.

Henry David Thoreau
March 13, 1842

j. lockhart

WOODCOCK

Philohela minor

The round borings of the woodcock in wet woodland fields are like signatures to his presence. This delicious game bird has long been a favorite of hunters from Canada to the Gulf. Often called "timber doodle" or "bog bird," the staple diet of this strange-looking nocturnal bird is the earthworm. This diet must be dug out of the moist earth. Nature has designed the strong, stout bill so it can be sunk to the nostrils. The tip of the upper mandible operates independently of the lower bill, and it is also flexible. With eyes set at the back of the head, food must be felt for rather than seen; however, the wide back vision does help in detecting enemies.

INTRODUCTION...

America's largest cat survives in only a few isolated areas of our country. Often called painter, puma, cougar, or mountain lion, this beautiful predator is to be found only in our true wilderness places. Conservationists plead for his continued existence so that a healthy balance of animals and plants will be maintained.

The kingfisher must have fish to survive. Poison and pollution in our streams have killed many of their fish, cutting back the kingfisher's range. Only where water is clean and quiet is this interesting bird still likely to be found.

*B*ecause I have always wanted to draw and paint, and because birds and animals have always fascinated me, it was inevitable that someday I would put the two together. I have had hours of pleasure observing the habits and ways of our wildlife, and I have sketched and photographed many bits of nature which attracted me. Much of that material has found its way into the paintings and drawings in this book.

This is not a book of analytical data that a biologist or ecologist might list, nor the facts that an ornithologist would record, but simply an accumulation of my nature paintings and drawings done over the past twenty-five years.

The paintings I have chosen are selective rather than comprehensive. I have not tried to include the infinite species of nature; rather, here is a sampling of things in nature that have appealed to me at various times. The writing must be modest. My aim has been a simple one: to show in my limited way the beauty of our American wildlife in their various natural habitats in the different seasons of the year.

As an artist my main purpose has been to depict the beauty of nature; however, over the years I have also felt strongly the need to point out that much of this natural beauty and

The screech owl, nature's flying mouse trap, is one of the most valuable allies of man, and one of the least understood. Insects, mice, and other small rodents comprise the greatest part of his diet, yet some people continue to shoot this little owl.

many of the birds and animals that I have painted are seriously threatened. I have tried to show many of the creatures that live upon this crowded land, and I hope that by creating a recognition of their beauty I may, in some small way, add to their chances for survival.

Our traditions and concept of the wilderness being of Western origin was deeply rooted in the words of the Bible. Man was created in the image of God, and all the things on earth were to be used and dominated. Man was to "have dominion over the fish of the sea, and over the fowl in the air, and over every living thing that moveth upon the earth." Western man followed this message so well that today there is little left in its natural state. To the Oriental, nature was viewed entirely differently, as one can sense in early Chinese scrolls and paintings. Man occupied only a small space in the great scenes that the Chinese artists drew. The mountains, the trees, and all of nature were pictured in scenes where man was non-existent, or only an insignificant part.

The English, from whom so much of our culture and ideas are derived, looked at nature in a different light. To them

Best-known member of the trout family, the beautiful rainbow trout seems quite adaptable when transplanted. Today he is in many parts of the world where water conditions are acceptable. A favorite among anglers, he is a good fighter when hooked. His spectacular leaps above water thrill any fisherman.

MOURNING DOVE

Zenaidura macroura

This shy, rather melancholy-sounding bird ranges from Quebec to Central America. There is often a pair nesting in an Austrian pine near my home, and their slow dirgelike song penetrates a surprising distance. The nests that I have observed are nothing more than a few loosely woven sticks—just enough to hold the usual two white eggs. When the nesting season approaches both birds make acrobatic flights above the tree tops, then sail with great accuracy to their perch. They show great devotion to each other, disregarding all other feathered friends. In the fall and winter the grain fields often attract large numbers of doves. Possessing a soft bill, they have to rely on other birds or animals to open an ear of corn.

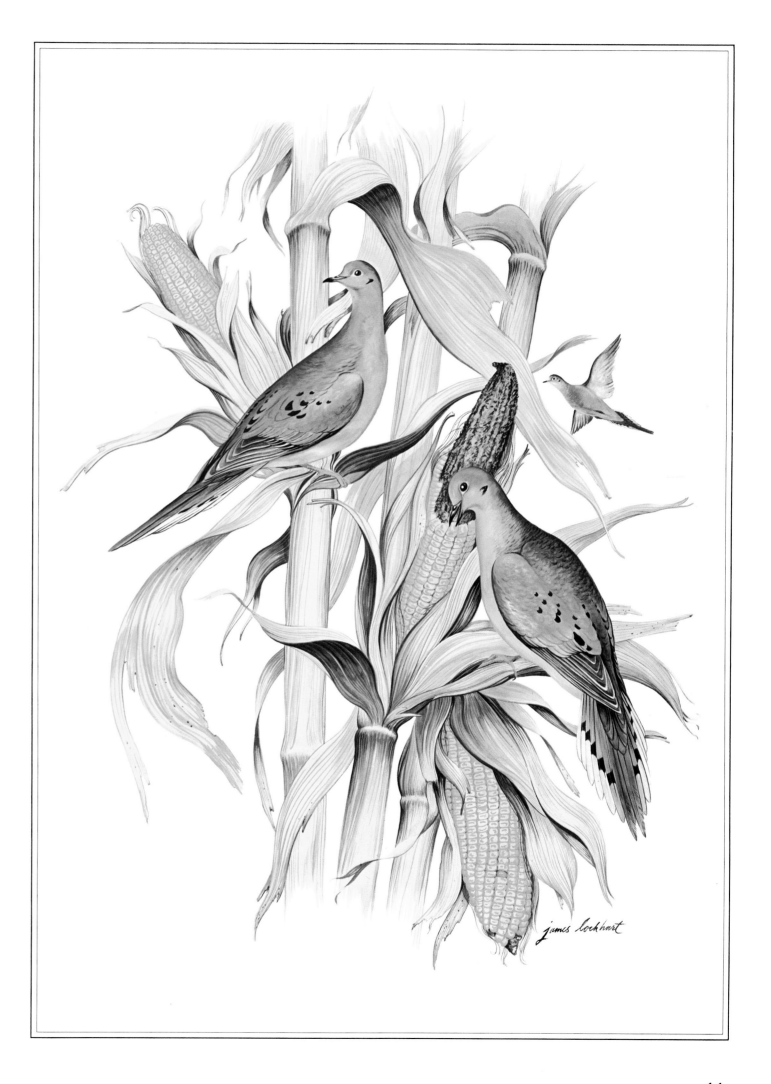

wilderness was something to be conquered, tamed, and put more into an orderly shape. The landscape was turned in a formal design and regimented. The neat, trimmed English garden was the ultimate example.

When our ancestors crossed the Atlantic they found a continent which was total wilderness occupied by wild beasts and primitive people. It was only natural that these people from England would set about attempting to tame the wilderness, and that a new England would be established here on our Eastern shores. But at the same time there were a few voices that began to be heard. There were artists, George Catlin and John James Audubon, who started to paint the landscapes and beautiful birds and animals which were living in this new land. Henry David Thoreau took up his pen and tried to make his young country aware of the beauty it possessed. By the time the messages of those early prophets became clear, America had little real wilderness to save.

The prairie chicken has been a victim of our civilization. In Illinois, the "Prairie State," farming machines destroyed thousands of eggs as man broke the prairies. Extinction of these birds can be delayed or perhaps stopped only if undisturbed grasslands are set aside for breeding sanctuaries.

Living almost entirely on grasshoppers, mice, and other insects, the beautiful small sparrow hawk has indirectly felt the effect of pesticides used in controlling insects near farming areas. When his food supply becomes contaminated, so does he.

John Muir's great effort saved some of the giant redwoods and the Yosemite Valley. A few years later Yellowstone National Park was created. All of America owes a great debt of gratitude for the foresight of the early conservationists, for today there is only about two percent of our land left that can be truly called natural wilderness, with the exception of Alaska.

There has been no time limit or deadline on my doing this book, just years of real pleasure; however, I do feel that there is a time limit on our remaining wild creatures and their habitat if they are to remain wild and free.

Take a walk into the woods, pause for a moment, and take the time to explore the forest floor and see nature's perfect factory. Here the processes of decay and renewal have been woven into a pattern that has maintained itself for centuries.

As a people we have conquered a continent; our frontiers exist no more, except in Alaska. No longer can we live off the land and move on. Preserve we must, for unlike our fathers, we can no longer move on to unspoiled areas. After many years of

The beautiful killdeers inhabit our pastures, plowed land, and golf courses. Usually four spotted eggs resembling smooth rocks are laid on the naked ground and are protected only by the killdeers' broken wing trick.

thoughtless waste, we must learn to preserve and reclaim our land, stop pollution, and save our wildlife for now man has the means to destroy not only nature, but himself. He also has the knowledge—and this is important—to devise ways to protect nature, and himself, for man is a vital part of nature.

As a people we have been masters at destroying what so many of us profess to like. Then we try desperately hard to restore it to the way it was before. Mother Nature seldom accommodates our wishes.

It would be hard to imagine our woods without birds or animal life, our streams and marshes without fish or waterfowl, or our fields without flowers. The patterns that nature has so skillfully designed must not be lost or damaged to the point that yet unborn generations can never experience the wonderful world that nature has planned. We must remember the cold, hard fact that extinction is final.

The beautiful coloring of the male scarlet tanager causes him to be sometimes confused with the cardinal, but a close comparison of the two birds shows that red feathers are their only similar features. The bright scarlet feathers of the male tanager are replaced in the fall by an inconspicuous olive-green and yellow plumage similar to the female.

The badger, when cornered, will fight with stubborn resistance, but it usually prefers to retreat to the safety of its underground burrow. A badger likes tracts of sandy soil where burrows can be easily constructed. This shy, nocturnal animal is seldom seen in its pursuit of mice, gophers, and ground squirrels, and is rarely surprised far away from his den.

WOOD DUCK

Aix sponsa

Most beautiful of all our waterfowl, the wood duck was first known to me in my native Arkansas as the "summer duck." Unlike most of our other ducks, this species confines itself exclusively to the North American continent, and has no counterpart in Asia or Europe. It nests in trees rather than on the ground, and is at home on a limb like a songbird. An abandoned hole of an owl or squirrel is all that is needed for a nesting site. Deep woods near a stream are preferred. This bird never quacks like other ducks; instead he has a musical call. The handsome drake stands guard to warn his mate of any impending danger. Exceedingly attached to their home, they will often return year after year to the same nest. The scientist who named this beautiful duck *Aix sponsa* — waterfowl in wedding dress — must have been aware of the affection this pair of ducks seem to demonstrate to each other.

Spring

You seldom see a ruffed grouse anywhere but in the deepest cover, except at times when they leave the thick timber and brush-grown areas to gravel up along an old logging trail. The "drumming" of the male is its most famous characteristic. Like the muffled beating of a drum, this remarkable bird-call of the male is his way of attracting the attention of the shy female. The drumming is heard most frequently in the spring around nesting time. On a spring fishing trip I was once lucky enough to observe a mother grouse with her covey of downy brown balls. When they spotted me, they scattered in every direction, and hid among the leaves so well I could not see a single one. The mother, acting like a crippled chicken, tried to lead us away from the area. I am sure a soft clucking call was all that was necessary as an all-clear signal to reunite the group.

I seek acquaintance with Nature—to know her moods and manners. Primitive nature is the most interesting to me. I take infinite pains to know all the phenomena of spring, for instance, thinking that I have here the entire poem, and then to my chagrin, I learn that it is but an imperfect copy that I possess and have read, that my ancestors have torn out many of the first leaves and grandest passages, and mutilated it in many places.

Henry David Thoreau
March 23, 1856

The ruby-throated hummingbird cannot be mistaken in our northern gardens, for it is our smallest bird neighbor. This little tropical jewel from Central America appears to be motionless while draining nectar from honeysuckle.

It is only a few steps from my studio to the ravine. From my vantage point it looks quite deep as it stretches down to Lake Michigan. It is not a great distance to the lake; it is actually a short walk along a path bordered by the rushing creek on one side and a brownish mattress of forest litter on the other. Carved out by glacier ice eons ago, this deep ravine and its twisting creek have been my inspiration and have supplied much of the flora and fauna for this book.

I have never really understood why I am drawn to the ravine unless it is because there I can practice the art of seeing, so important to an artist. Perhaps, I might get a glimpse of a wood duck, or a new flock of birds on their migration north. At times the creek would be up, washing untold silt into Lake Michigan; yet a few weeks later it would be so sluggish that a crayfish would stand out as I would stare at the sandy bottom. What interesting structure in the wings of a dead dragonfly or the intricate beauty of some weed all waiting to have some eyes focused on their fragile beauty.

The ravine became part of my leisure as well as my work; yet this task has been one of my greatest pleasures, for seeing is the first step towards creation. The art of seeing is a disciplined effort that cannot be taught; it must be practiced.

The red-winged blackbird is one of the first arrivals from the South in the early spring. Marsh visitors in every state are familiar with his "con, quer-ee" call, and his bright scarlet shoulder patches.

VIRGINIA and SORA RAIL

Rallus limicola
Porzana carolina

If I had never duck hunted, I probably would
have never become aware of the rail family. As boys
we called all rail birds "mud hens," never recognizing
the many different types that lived hidden in the sedges
and bulrushes. All rails are short of wing, and have a
feeble or fluttering flight when they are flushed in the
marsh, yet they are capable of migrating from New York
to Florida. The small sora rail can move through a maze
of grass without causing a blade to move, and it is a rare
sight to see one exposed. A few years back I saw one in
the shrubbery next to my home. Thinking it was injured,
I was attempting to pick it up when it flew straight
upward and headed for the ravine. If you have ever
heard a sweet "ker-wee, ker-wee" or "ki-ki-ki" you can
be sure you have heard a rail.

In my travels to Alaska, our deserts in the Southwest, the bayous and marshes of my native South, and elsewhere, I have tried to portray parts of America that are still wild. There I saw the grizzly bear, the moose, the bald eagle, and others long gone from my ravine; but were these any more wild than the creatures who live and hide in my ravine? When I walk into their domain, the juncos fly for cover, the jays and crows scream their alarm, rabbits run for cover, squirrels dash for their holes, and all else vanish into this little part of wild America. Why do they run and hide, I have often thought? The answer must be because they are still wild.

At times the ravine is a roofless tunnel; at other times the sky is closed out by a canopy of green or bright red and gold with overlapping branches. Trees struggle up the steep bank and over the crest. That this is an old forest is evidenced by the fact that nature has replaced most of the aspens and poplars with massive oaks, maples, and a variety of other trees and bushes. These trees and plants each play a part in providing food and shelter for many of the birds and animals that I have painted.

Detail of Bald Eagle painting
See Spring print section for complete painting

When the last snow has melted and the birds have stripped the last bright red berries from the barberry, I watch for the first signs of new life.

When the smelly skunk cabbage thrusts its spikes through the frosted soil, or a little later when the bloodroot or the hepatica are reborn, they stir a deep feeling within that life is being renewed. The cycle of seed to seedpod is about to start all over again. When the ravine banks seem to be snow-covered with white trillium, broken only by small patches of adder's-tongue, wake-robin, or yellow and purple violets in all their delicate beauty, then no calendar is needed to announce spring.

Even though barn owls have accepted quarters in barns and other outbuildings of man, a hollow tree remains their favorite home. They are one of nature's best mousers, and a valuable asset around any farm.

The colorful brook trout has disappeared from much of its former range. They must have cold, clean water to survive, and transplanting them has not been too successful in many areas. Brookies have long been a favorite for those who enjoy the skill of fly fishing.

At this time of year sunlight streams through the still naked branches of the oaks and maples; the wild honeysuckles alone show green. The stream is full, still draining the last winter runoff snow. Without this marriage of woods and water the ravine would be just a large gully—with both it is a retreat for many small animals and birds. Raccoons, squirrels, possums, groundhogs, red foxes, chipmunks, weasels, and others exist together among the light-green ferns and brush. Not too long ago the whitetail deer was seen, but now he is gone along with the bobcats, bears, and other large animals that have given way to man's encroachment.

My first nature painting was born here. Even today when I travel to distant places to gather material foreign to the soil and climate of my ravine, I will never forget the small brook, the frisky chipmunks with their network of tunnels, the red fox den, the wood duck who nested in the hollow tree by the brook, and the many wildflowers which thrive in this moist, acid soil of my ravine. Perhaps as I look back I could have found a lifetime of material and pleasure right in my own back yard. There are so many things still to be painted—and spring is the season of hope.

The American mink swims and dives with ease in its search for aquatic food. Remarkably strong and agile for such a small animal, a trout or mallard is not safe from this solitary member of the weasel family. The mink, though semi-aquatic, will sometimes travel long distances from water in search of an unprotected hen house.

The following reproductions of paintings are a selection of subjects depicting some of the best known birds and animals of North America. The paintings were primarily painted with casein paint on board. Approximate size of each painting is 30 inches by 40 inches.

WHITE-TAILED DEER — *Odocoileus virginianus*

COMMON LOON — *Gavia immer*

RED-WING — *Agelaius phoeniceus*

GRIZZLY BEAR — *Ursus horribilis*

AMERICAN EGRET — *Casmerodius albus*

WILSON'S SNIPE — *Gallinago gallinago*

CALIFORNIA QUAIL — *Lophortyx californicus*

SCREECH OWL — *Otus asio*

RACCOONS — *Procyon lotor*

HOUSE WREN — *Troglodytes aedon*

AMERICAN WOODCOCK — *Philohela minor*

TRUMPETER SWAN — *Cygnus buccinator*

The combination of their bright splash of color and their beautiful song in my windbreak is reason enough to hold my interest in the cardinals year round. He is one of our permanent residents.

WHITE-TAILED DEER (Odocoileus virginianus)

COMMON LOON (Gavia immer)

RED-WING (Agelaius phoeniceus)

GRIZZLY BEAR (Ursus horribilis)

AMERICAN EGRET (Casmerodius albus)

WILSON'S SNIPE (Gallinago gallinago)

CALIFORNIA QUAIL (Lophortyx californicus)

SCREECH OWL (Otus asio)

RACCOONS (Procyon lotor)

HOUSE WREN (Troglodytes aedon)

AMERICAN WOODCOCK (Philohela minor)

TRUMPETER SWAN (Cygnus buccinator)

Summer

Since the dawn of history, man has lived in close association with migratory waterfowl. He has relied upon their abundance for a major part of his food. There is nothing that brings out the sporting instinct or stirs the imagination of a man more than seeing the long-necked Canada goose flying in the familiar wedge-shaped formation across the autumn sky. In my lifetime, this once common sight has become far less frequent, but far-sighted sportsmen and other conservation groups have now reversed this declining trend. With sensible and rigid hunting regulations and new breeding reserves, the Canada goose, as well as other waterfowl, shows great promise of holding its own in this crowded world. The old gander I have pictured makes a good lookout, for he possesses one of the keenest eyesights in nature, and it is rare, indeed, when this sentinel is caught off guard.

Now is the time [to] observe the leaves, so fair in color and so perfect in form. I stood over a sprig of choke-cherry, with fair and perfect glossy green obovate and serrate leaves, in the woods this p.m., as if it were a rare flower. Now the various forms of oak leaves in the sprout-lands, wet-glossy, as if newly painted green and varnished, attract me.

Henry David Thoreau
June 4, 1854

In summer the ravine seems almost mine alone. When the early
wildflowers have died, the canopy of leaves almost closes in the
ravine and shuts out the sky. Only a few now enter this green world.

Each season has its joys and pleasures, and one swiftly
changes to another. The brook is now not in such a hurry to reach
the lake, and the birds do not want to betray their nests; their
spring songs have given way to warnings only to chase away a too-
close intruder. All this concealment has been planned by nature.
Now is the time to observe the little things. Each leaf with its
glossy texture and delicate pattern, the Queen Anne's lace, so
beautiful in its summer dress, the emerald moss, the white
leathery underside and dark green topside of the aspen—all these
wait to inspire those who take the time for a close look.

The fringe of the woods is a pattern of unexpected things.
There flourish the jack-in-the-pulpit, wild strawberries, hawthorns,
and crab apples, all showing their young green fruit. It happens
so swiftly, so suddenly that should one miss a month he finds
that the whole picture has been changed and been replaced by
something else standing out for attention.

With a glossy black and white body and a
bright red head, this bird is the most conspicuous
member of the woodpecker family. The
red-head has too often been the target of rifles
and slingshots. Their diet consists mostly of
beetles, grubs, and acorns, but they will
not pass up cherries or ripe apples for a treat.

Once hunted for his hide, the peccary is no longer
slaughtered to make gloves and leather jackets. Our only
native wild pig will eat anything from cactus to rattlesnakes,
with acorns a special favorite.

RACCOON

Procyon lotor

Raccoons thrive in most environments, as many suburban residents will verify. The painting to the right depicts a burnt-out Southern swamp scene, with an arrowleaf plant going to seed. Lotor means "a washer" in Latin, and that seems to be a quaint characteristic of this talented masked animal. One of the most valuable and plentiful fur-bearing animals of North America, the "coon," as he was called in the South, was harvested intensively. Formerly, in the states of the lower Mississippi valley his skins were used as a circulating medium. Today, he seems to be able to take care of himself whether he is in a Southern bayou or in New York's Central Park. With his talented hands Brer Coon is one mammal that nature has designed to take civilization in stride.

The raccoon family is limited to two members—the raccoon and the ring-tailed cat, which has a restricted range in desert lands near the Mexican border. My association has only been with several species of the raccoon *(Procyon lotor)*. There is a considerable variation in color as well as size. The raccoon is often referred to as the brother of the bear, due to a resemblance in build and in the full-soled naked feet, and also because it walks in a plantigrade manner. I have tried to capture the restless, inquisitive, and prying characteristics of this charming mammal in this portrait.

Detail of Raccoon Painting on Page 51

In the marshy spots grow the wild lavender and the wild iris with its graceful arching leaves. This is the time of sweet scents, to be followed by the almost flowerless months of midsummer, for then dense leaves shut out most of the sunlight and the ravine goes into the silent drowsiness of dragging summer. This is a time when mind and body can rest in the ravine. Away from the fierce hot sunlight of the outer world, the quiet and stillness beckon. Nature makes you walk slowly and observe, for all the quickness of pace is gone in the summer heat. The ferns have lost their youth and begin to brown from the bottom; only those close to the stream stand green and erect. Umbrellas of fungi open near a rotting log, and one can smell strange, dank odors after a humid rain.

Over past summers my many encounters with the black-masked Jesse James of the animal world have centered around my patio fountain. But loving wildlife and the outdoors, I would not bring myself to paint the raccoon in such a civilized setting.

This masked rascal is native only to North and Central America, and he takes man and his works in stride. They live in my ravine, but can thrive near civilization. Taken young, a raccoon makes a delightful pet.

Having grown up near Louisiana, I was well aware of America's number-one fur bearer, the muskrat. This lowly marsh rodent is prominent in the fur industry and is trapped from the Arctic to the Rio Grande. Active day and night, the muskrat sometimes eats his own dome-shaped house. Cattails and pond weeds are favorite foods.

Faster than a race horse, the pronghorn antelope is America's swiftest animal. Not a true antelope, it is the sole member of the American family Antilocapridae. Once seemingly doomed, the pronghorn has been brought back to greatly increased numbers on our Western plains by effective conservation and limited hunting.

Where corn is grown in abundance and a stand of timber provides cover, raccoons seem to multiply in spite of hunting pressure. If he lives near a stream or swamp, a raccoon will fish or hunt for mussels which he can open with remarkable skill. He will climb, wade, or swim to satisfy his tastes. There is one trait the raccoon possesses whether he lives in New England or in a Southern swamp, and that is washing his food. He will sometimes go hungry rather than eat unwashed food. Restless and inquisitive, this intelligent and engaging bear-like creature has remained my favorite since youth.

During late summer the ravine slowly becomes alive again. The chipmunks are the first to take notice that the fall winds are not far off. With the nesting period over, the birds are no longer silent, and there is a general restlessness in the ravine. With the summer heat in retreat, the miracle of change once again commences. One must now take a closer look, for the soft shades of greens are starting to show the delicate patterns of yellow, red, and brown. A dying leaf can be beautiful if one will only take an intent look. The thistle is waiting for the autumn winds to scatter its seeds. One does not have to be an artist to see that nature is once again slowly transforming the ravine into one of its most beautiful seasons.

No one can mistake the long tail of the pintail drake for any other species of duck. One of the most wide-ranging of all North American river and pond ducks, the pintail feeds mostly on pondweeds, sedges and grains. Clean water is necessary for their survival.

The following twelve paintings reflect summer — the time of year when most of us see wildlife. Our impressions of the color of most animals are formed during this period; however, most observers are aware that color varies and is very fleeting within plant species as well as with animals. Black bears may not be black — some are cinnamon, brown, bluish, or even white — and so it is with many other species.

RED FOX — *Vulpes fulva*

WOOD DUCK — *Aix sponsa*

ROBIN — *Turdus migratorius*

AMERICAN BLACK BEAR — *Ursus americanus*

ATLANTIC SALMON — *Salmo salar*

BALD EAGLE — *Haliaeetus leucocephalus*

COTTONTAIL RABBIT — *Sylvilagus floridanus*

ALLIGATOR — *Alligator mississipiensis*

FLICKER — *Colaptes auratus*

AMERICAN MOOSE — *Alces alces*

MOCKINGBIRD — *Mimus polyglottos*

BIGHORN SHEEP — *Ovis canadensis*

At the turn of the century the snowy egret almost disappeared from the American scene. Plume hunters invaded the aeries for feathers until only a few colonies remained. Today, with their numbers restored, no other bird offers a better example of proof that conservation can be made to work.

RED FOX (Vulpes fulva)

WOOD DUCK (Aix sponsa)

ROBIN (Turdus migratorius)

AMERICAN BLACK BEAR (Ursus americanus)

ATLANTIC SALMON (Salmo salar)

BALD EAGLE (Haliaeetus leucocephalus)

COTTONTAIL RABBIT (Sylvilagus floridanus)

ALLIGATOR (Alligator mississipiensis)

FLICKER (Colaptes auratus)

AMERICAN MOOSE (Alces alces)

MOCKINGBIRD (Mimus polyglottos)

BIGHORN SHEEP (Ovis canadensis)

Fall

In the world of children's literature, no other animal has been a greater favorite than the rabbit. The rabbit's breath-taking escapes from larger enemies have been retold for children in all parts of the world. However, in real nature, these escapes are often never accomplished. When pursued, a rabbit will almost always run in a wide circle, seldom leaving the area he knows best. He is extremely clever at throwing a dog off his trail by retracing his steps, and he has other tricks which he has had to learn to survive. Sometimes these tricks succeed and sometimes they do not. Unlike Brer Rabbit in the tales of Uncle Remus, not all rabbits can flee for safety to the dense protection of a briar patch or into a ravine.

The brilliant autumnal colors are red and yellow and the various tints, hues, and shades of these. Blue is reserved to be the color of the sky, but yellow and red are the colors of the earth-flower. Every fruit on ripening, and just before its fall, acquires a bright tint. So do the leaves: so the sky before the end of the day, and year near its setting.

Henry David Thoreau
October 24, 1858

The flying squirrel, one of nature's best gliders, is seldom seen. Strictly nocturnal, it is a docile and gentle creature. When they cut the great hardwood forests of southern Arkansas, I used to see these squirrels leap out of the timber and flee in all directions. When captured they made wonderful pets, and were very fond of the wild pecans that we gathered each fall.

When the warblers flit through branches of yellow-gold and orange, and the brook reflects the warm glow of the hillside, nature has painted another new picture in the ravine. The squirrels and chipmunks work with intense industry to store acorns and seeds before winter overtakes them. Could we have a natural forest without these industrious rodents, always planting and storing the acorns and seeds, then forgetting many so that they may sprout next season through the forest floor?

One late afternoon as I rested on a log I noticed a moving branch on one of the pines. I could see nothing, and the wind was calm, yet this one branch continued to move. Finally the whole picture became clear; a mouse no larger than a pine cone was taking seeds from an open cone. My day was made, for another idea had been born in the ravine. I could hardly wait to sketch the picture on paper.

At this time of year, beautiful and bountiful as it is, one is constantly reminded in these woods of the fragile relationship between our animal and plant life. We are reminded how closely they are linked together in a delicate balance. A poor growing season of plants, nuts, and fruits affects the animals' survival. Large or small, the plants and animals are all linked in a chain.

The white-footed mouse, with his black shining eyes, is one of nature's neatest and smallest mammals. This immaculate small inhabitant of our woodlands possesses a gentle disposition; and falls prey to many birds, snakes, and other carnivores.

RING-NECKED PHEASANT

Phasianus colchicus torquatus

In the Midwest the pheasant is perhaps the most popular upland gamebird. He seems to have filled a void in the many states where the ruffed grouse, or bobwhite, is absent or in short supply. Successfully introduced into western Oregon in 1881 from China, this immigrant is now common over much of the northern parts of the United States and southern Canada. Just recently one walked up to my studio door, looked in, and casually strutted away. But when the pumpkin and the corn turn yellow, he becomes a different bird, cautious and wary. Despite his brilliant plumage, he can lose himself in amazingly scant cover. Give him a few tufts of grass, and one has to almost step on him to locate him. Several years ago I saw a whole marsh come alive at daybreak with much flapping of wings and crowing. This commotion stopped only after the pheasants left the marsh to feed in the nearby cornfields.

Once abundant over most of the country, this noble gamebird was almost hunted to extinction. Only in inaccessible pockets of bottom land and in the mountains did he survive. Only the most cautious and suspicious birds were left, and today the wild turkey remains one of the most cunning, wary, and almost unapproachable birds. Starting at the earliest sign of dawn, while still on his perch high off the ground, the gobbler will utter his call. The hens all roost in a different tree nearby. When the turkey is feeding, he scratches and turns leaves over and disturbs the area in a way that reminds one of chickens feeding. As they feed, the gobbler, with head held high, always seems to be on the alert. That is the scene I have tried to capture in my painting. In spite of their cunning and their great cleverness, the wild turkeys still need man's protection if they are not to pass into extinction. Today, with protection, they are making progress.

Detail of Turkey painting
See Fall print section for complete painting

If one link breaks, disaster can result. The plants are the first link in the chain. The mass of leaves, twigs, and other debris that litters the ravine floor is ground up by the beetles, grubs, and other insects, returning nutrients to the soil. The fungi—toadstools and mushrooms—break down other dead plants into material for a new generation of flora all waiting to be reborn in the spring.

Since Aesop told his fable of the fox tricking the crow out of his cluster of grapes twenty-six centuries ago, the fox has symbolized guile and cunning. This little creature has been pursued with bow-and-arrow, traps, and firearms for centuries, and yet he is very much with us today. In fact the den I have painted is in the ravine less than a block away from my studio. The fox will live so close to man, it sometimes appears he is seeking man's affection like his domestic cousin the dog.

The red fox is the most common fox of North America. His rusty red coat, his large bushy white-tipped tail and his black legs distinguish him easily from his cousin, the gray fox. Grays keep more to the deep woods, and they have not learned to outwit man as well as the red fox. The red fox is not as large as most people think; he weighs only about twelve pounds. To see him coursing across a frozen field with his tail in a horizontal position is a beautiful sight.

Protected from end to end in bony armor, the armadillo was named "little fellow in armor" by the early Spanish explorers. He grubs mostly at night, and being related to the anteater, he relishes ants, spiders, and even scorpions. Originally seen only in the Rio Grande country, they are now as far east as Florida, and they have even appeared in central Arkansas.

The Eastern chipmunk never seems to stop harvesting. With both cheeks full, he seems to always be on the go. Nuts, grain, strawberries, and even the small cherry tomatoes in my garden are never safe from this compulsive little squirrel. Full of vigor and with tail held high, he dashes back and forth across my yard to the safety of the wooded ravine and continues his labors as long as I remain quiet.

The service of this little wild canine in rodent control alone should justify his existence. He has demonstrated his ability to live near man and to learn by studying our ways and actions. The more we understand this remarkable creature, the more likely we will not think of him as part of a fable or legend, but accept him as a valuable asset in our environment.

This situation has threatened our deer. Where natural predators such as the mountain lion, wolf, or lynx have been eliminated, deer populations often explode. Overgrazing results, and their food supply is diminished or destroyed. Disease and starvation are the result.

Many books have been published about America's geographic splendors, its mountains, its great rivers, its deserts and fertile plains. But in contemplating the hugeness of our domain we sometimes lose sight of the small areas and the creatures that inhabit the small areas close at home. Standing on the crest of my hillside admiring the autumnal glow of yellow and scarlet with touches of green, I hope the ravine will always offer such inspiring beauty and that the sugar maples, the white and red oaks, and the wild apple and cherry will always glow brightly for those who have discovered the secret of seeing.

Possessing marvelous diving and swimming ability, the hooded merganser lives mainly on fish, with an occasional frog or small shellfish. Like the wood duck, the merganser builds a nest of leaves and grasses lined with down from the mother's breast.

The selection of birds and animals portraying fall are ones I know best. As a boy I grew up in an area where game was plentiful and hunting was a way of life. Today, I do most of my hunting with a high-speed color camera, which I use as a help in my work; but I would like to think that hours of observation and study, and one's artistic skill, will never be replaced by the lens.

WILD TURKEY — *Meleagris gallopavo*

EASTERN CHIPMUNK — *Tamias striatus*

BLACK-CAPPED CHICKADEE — *Parus atricapillus*

CANADA GOOSE — *Branta canadensis*

RED FOX — *Vulpes fulva*

BLUE JAY — *Cyanocitta cristata*

CROW — *Corvus brachyrhynchos*

GREEN-WINGED TEAL — *Anas carolinensis*

BISON or BUFFALO — *Bison bison*

AVOCET — *Recurvirostra americana*

SOUTHERN FLYING SQUIRREL — *Glaucomys volans*

GREAT HORNED OWL — *Bubo virginianus*

Some say the frolicsome and mischievous red squirrel possesses fewer virtues and more vices than any other animal in the woods. He is an acknowledged nuisance at times, yet it is hard to keep from liking this little forester.

WILD TURKEY (Meleagris gallopavo)

EASTERN CHIPMUNK (Tamias striatus)

BLACK-CAPPED CHICKADEE (Parus atricapillus)

CANADA GOOSE (Branta canadensis)

RED FOX (Vulpes fulva)

BLUE JAY (Cyanocitta cristata)

CROW (Corvus brachyrhynchos)

GREEN-WINGED TEAL (Anas carolinensis)

BISON or BUFFALO (Bison bison)

AVOCET (Recurvirostra americana)

SOUTHERN FLYING SQUIRREL (Glaucomys volans)

GREAT HORNED OWL (Bubo virginianus)

Winter

The crow is a rowdy, avaricious, noisy, large, and conspicuous black bird, blessed with native intelligence second to none in the bird world. His black silhouette and bold flight patterns are beautiful as he flaps slowly across a cold, gray winter sky. When most other birds leave their Northern homes, the crow stays, yet his presence does not seem to be greeted with joy. He infuriates the farmer by eating his crops, and he destroys small game and songbirds, as well as millions of duck eggs in our waterfowl breeding grounds. With a record such as this, one can hardly expect the crow to have a host of friends. Nothing seems to escape his observant eye, and he is so innately suspicious that catching him off guard is seldom accomplished. He will boldly fly to the most conspicuous perch in broad daylight, and then call to all within hearing distance. His intelligence and high social order ensure that the crow is not in any present danger.

The thin snow now driving from the north and lodging on my coat consists of those beautiful star crystals, . . . Nature is full of genius, full of the divinity; so that not a snowflake escapes its fashioning hand.

. . . The same law that shapes the earth-star shapes the snow-star. As surely as the petals of a flower are fixed, each of these countless snow-stars come whirling to earth, pronouncing thus, with emphasis, the number six.

Henry David Thoreau
January 5, 1856

All that summer and fall have tried to conceal, winter has opened up and revealed. The skeleton branches of the deciduous trees have shed their cover on the frosted floor. Now the ravine is left to its few permanent residents. The robins, warblers, and others have long migrated. Only the jays, cardinals, and a few others are left. The crows are always near, roosting in a few large spruce trees, and making odd clucking calls interspersed with shrill notes. These large black birds seem to love winter. I love to see them buck a strong north wind: at times they appear to be motionless; then they suddenly turn and sail with the wind.

The stillness in the ravine is absolute now, because the creek is frozen over. No water hurries to find Lake Michigan. The creaking of ice as some restless limbs rub against each other breaks this otherwise dead silence. Only a close and patient observer can see and tell that the ravine is still alive. Now and then the jays warn all within earshot in this small part of the world that an intruder is near. There are telltale signatures in the snow near the entrances to the burrows and dens. The cottontail has left his tracks in the snow, and the nearby shrubs have been neatly pruned. All the tender shoots have a chisel cut, for there are no green plants or grass to eat.

Resident and wanderer of the Arctic, the polar bear is the
most determinedly carnivorous of all the bears. Stalking like
a hungry leopard, he captures seals, walrus, and fish.
Even a stranded whale is not safe from this white ghost.

Best known of the river and pond ducks, the mallard is perhaps the duck dearest to the sportsman's heart. The glossy green head with a white collar around the neck and the curved black tail feathers are unmistakable identification marks of the drake.

Quite a few years ago I was looking for a different plant to put in a rabbit painting. On going to the ravine I spotted a startled cottontail dash away from a mayapple plant. When I examined the area, one bite of the ripe yellow fruit was missing. I will never know if that rabbit made that bite, but I do know that I dug up the plant and brought it into my studio where I painted the scene that I saw.

The wood mice, shrews, and even mink etch their presence on the snow, and I have observed that the fox is well aware of their presence. The woodchuck and a few others sleep through all this winter beauty. At times the trees are frosted dead white in nature's beautiful embroidery; other times these same trees are bent and drooping with the weight of a wet snow—beautiful again in their prayer-like posture. The evergreens have a character all their own as their boughs curve with perfection, until the wet snow slips with a muffled sound. Occasionally a woodpecker breaks the silence as he drills rapidly. I wonder what he might find to eat in this frozen world as he thrusts his spear-like tongue in the hole he has just hammered in the trunk of a dead tree. The chickadees with their black caps, the slate-colored juncos, and the occasional nuthatches all seem to me to have an easier life in their quests for leftover seeds as they nervously go from branch to branch.

I have never been a skier or winter sport enthusiast, but I am always attracted to the ravine after a new snow. The snow is then so clean and pure, the trees are all powdered white with billions of star-like crystals—each quite different. All evidence of man's intrusion is covered by soft drifts. One cannot help but feel peace within in this church-like atmosphere. Under this nourishing blanket of snow the wild ginger, bluebells, wild phlox, spring beauty, and others are just waiting for the call of spring. In the ravine the seasons have performed a perfect cycle. Thoreau wrote long ago that the natural and the civilized worlds must live together or perish separately.

As an artist I am aware, as are many nature observers, that the preservation and protection of nature's wonders are vitally important to all who live on this planet. Since we have but one Earth on which to live, how fortunate we are that this one has so much natural beauty, so many infinite varieties of plants and wildlife. The beautiful mountains with their forests and rivers, the grassy plains, the deep oceans, and our deserts—all are a part of a world which requires continuing vigilance and protection.

The bluegill is certainly one of the best known of our sunfishes. It is one of our most widely distributed species, and is found in ponds, streams, and lakes. As a pan fish it is delicious, and it also ranks high among anglers as a game fish.

BOBWHITE

Colinus virginianus

The bobwhite named himself by his call, and one has to feel happier for having heard his exuberant whistle in the spring. Often the male will remain out of the group as a guard to warn the covey of any danger. Should trouble come, the covey will explode in all directions with a loud whr-r-r-r. Even when you know bobwhites are present and you are prepared for their flight the noise is startling. Once the danger has passed, a clear, sweet call unites the family, and one by one the birds form their covey. All farmers love the bobwhite for he is constantly at work eating insects and worms that are destructive to crops. However, since spraying has become common, his ranks have been thinned by poisoned worms. The injurious practice of spraying, coupled with the fox and other natural enemies, has eliminated this great game bird from many areas. Since he always lives close to his place of birth, his continued presence depends on the protection and care given by the people who share his community.

Several years ago, when part of my property was beginning to erode into the ravine, I started piling up limbs and branches to hold the soil. It did not occur to me that I was helping create a perfect camouflage entrance for a woodchuck den, but a woodchuck thought of it. Often late in the afternoon I have noticed the woodchuck family feeding near the brush pile. They would seldom come out into the open yard unless the clover was blooming. On close inspection I found several trails all leading out from the brush pile. Woodchucks have been known to wreak havoc with gardens, but this family stayed entirely away from my flower and vegetable plot. I was content to keep it that way.

When I return to my boyhood home, somehow I always find the time to go out to the back fence to see if the wild rose bush that I planted as a boy has survived a few more years. Are the purple violets that I transplanted from the wet delta still there?

If one will take only a few minutes to look closely and study the artistry of nature, be it such a familiar thing as a dried or withered leaf, the opening of a milkweed pod after the first frost, or the beauty of the petals on a wildflower, he will take the first step toward an appreciation of the wonderful aspects of things that cannot be found in our asphalt-paved cities.

Taking over and often enlarging deserted prairie dog burrows is the habit of the gnome-like burrowing owl. He is a valuable ally of the rancher, for he eliminates mice, gophers, and other rodents.

BROWN PELICAN
Pelecanus occidentalis

Originally found from North Carolina and British Columbia to Brazil, the brown pelican in recent years has been on the decline in numbers. Pesticides again have been blamed for the problem, and since the ban on D.D.T., there seems to have been an increase of these birds along our Southern coastline. Louisiana, called the Pelican State, has had to transplant birds in the hope that colonies can be reestablished. Some years ago when I visited Pelican Island, a refuge in the Indian River of Florida, there were so many birds congregated on the mangroves that the trees seemed almost bare of foliage. The terrific force with which the pelican dives into the sea is amazing, but more amazing is the fact that no injury seems to result. The large pouch is used as a dip net and not as a carrier of food. Northern visitors to our Southern coastline constantly marvel at this ungainly inhabitant.

The winter season is when our land seems most quiet and still, often covered with a blanket of stainless white. The trees have leafless boughs, the meadows are dead and barren, yet much of our non-migrating wildlife must somehow survive on sparse buds, bark, and seeds. I have tried to portray nature in subtle colors, accented by the few bright chromatic colors found in this season.

CARDINAL — *Cardinalis cardinalis*

BOBWHITE — *Colinus virginianus*

GREAT GRAY OWL — *Strix nebulosa*

WHITE-TAILED DEER — *Odocoileus virginianus*

WILD TURKEY — *Meleagris gallopavo*

GRAY or TIMBER WOLF — *Canis lupus*

BUFFLEHEAD — *Bucephala albeola*

RED-SHOULDERED HAWK — *Buteo lineatus*

PRONGHORN — *Antilocapra americana*

AMERICAN ELK or WAPITI — *Cervus canadensis*

RUFFED GROUSE — *Bonasa umbellus*

MULE DEER — *Odocoileus hemionus*

The European partridge, perhaps better known as the Hungarian partridge, has been successfully introduced into some parts of the United States and Canada. My first experience with these birds was in the grain fields of Saskatchewan. Their great speed on the wing makes them an excellent game bird, and they seem to be able to thrive in areas where other game birds are absent.

CARDINAL (Cardinalis cardinalis)

BOBWHITE (Colinus virginianus)

GREAT GRAY OWL (Strix nebulosa)

WHITE-TAILED DEER (Odocoileus virginianus)

WILD TURKEY (Meleagris gallopavo)

GRAY or TIMBER WOLF (Canis lupus)

BUFFLEHEAD (Bucephala albeola)

RED-SHOULDERED HAWK (Buteo lineatus)

PRONGHORN (Antilocapra americana)

AMERICAN ELK or WAPITI (Cervus canadensis)

RUFFED GROUSE (Bonasa umbellus)

MULE DEER (Odocoileus hemionus)

BALD EAGLE

Haliaëetus leucocephalus

The freedom and independence of our young nation have been symbolized by the bald eagle since early colonial days. This handsome bird has been designed into our paper money, coins, and architecture. Wherever the American flag flies he is usually found perched atop its mast. At the present time, our great national emblem is in serious danger from the pressures of civilization and pesticides. Only a few sections of America can now claim his presence. His enormous size and majestic bearing make his appearance a moment of excitement whenever he is seen. A swift bird with superior strength and keen sight, he has man alone to fear. Once a mate is selected, eagles stay together for life, and return to the same nesting place year after year. Their homesites, or aeries, are defended with fierce devotion. I am convinced that our forefathers chose the right bird to symbolize our new country, and that we should aid our nature societies to protect this truly American bird. If we do perhaps he can continue to ride the air currents, symbolizing freedom and strength.

Perhaps many of us are so busy that we are not yet sufficiently aware that so much of our natural beauty and so many of our animals and plants are actually threatened with extinction. Each year much of our wildlife and wilderness is being lost to the bulldozer and the chain saw. Almost every day of the year and in every state of our Union, a swamp or marsh is being drained, timber is wiped out by the saw or by a careless fire, a stream is changed by pollution or dredged for some purpose. This rapid altering of our environment is happening not only here at home, but in distant deserts, swamps, jungles, and even in remote parts of our planet. With these swift changes in our environment, extinction is threatening many of our wild creatures. New poisons, traps, poachers, and even fishermen with electronic gadgets, are taking their toll of the wild creatures of this planet.

One does not have to be an artist to observe that conservation came too late for some of our wildlife, and that the emblem of our great nation—personifying freedom and strength—is fighting for his right to survive. The bald eagle, as well as many others, desperately needs our help.

BEAVER
Castor canadensis

Largest and certainly one of the most intelligent North American rodents, the beaver uses webbed hind feet and a flat scaly tail in tireless dam building efforts. Beavers, like man, work and live in communities. They demonstrate teamwork, and appear to practice strict rules. They work for conservation by building ponds and canals as if they were hired by the conservation department. Waterfowl and fish are most grateful for this work. Beavers build a whole series of smaller dams so that a heavy spring runoff does not put too much pressure on the main dam which contains their home. Like most animals of the forest, the beaver is not without enemies. If a bobcat comes near, a beaver will flap his broad tail on the water to signal danger. This marvelous tail also serves as a rudder when he swims, and a balance when he works. The early trading of his valuable fur helped open up a large part of our continent; but as a result, he was almost wiped out. Dedicated nature lovers and sound conservation practice have worked in his favor, and the beaver is no longer a threatened species.

It seems unimportant to many people that a particular species is eliminated from an area, yet the presence of that bird or animal or plant may play an important role in nature's balance, and could quite possibly have a direct effect upon mankind's own habitat. In our own West we witnessed a situation in which predators were killed off by man, allowing the mule deer to multiply rapidly. They became so numerous in an area that they overbrowsed their range, and turned it into a desert.

A mother bobcat usually hunts in early morning or evening unless she is training her kits. Wildcats seldom hunt in the daytime. A hollow tree or a cavern among the rocks is usually the place where a den is most likely to be found.

WILDCAT
Felis rufa

Very wary of man and now seldom seen outside of a zoo, the wildcat usually prowls at night. For the most part these stub-tailed cats hunt alone. Toes with soft cushions enable them to move quietly, and armed with deadly retracting claws these felines are very effective at hunting small game. Their hunting tactic is to be in ambush and spring out with lightning speed on the prey. When cornered by dogs or men, or especially when they have young, they show why they have well earned the reputation, "He can lick his weight in wildcats." Looking much like a large, overgrown house cat, the wildcat can thrive wherever there is enough cover and wherever he is left alone by man. When a bobcat is on the prowl, he sometimes utters a chilling wild scream. Apparently his object is to startle any small creature into betraying his hiding place. Even though he is useful in keeping rabbits and other destructive rodents in check, the wildcat has never been welcomed by man.

james lockhart

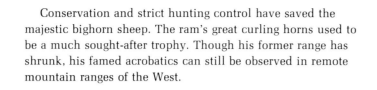

Conservation and strict hunting control have saved the majestic bighorn sheep. The ram's great curling horns used to be a much sought-after trophy. Though his former range has shrunk, his famed acrobatics can still be observed in remote mountain ranges of the West.

We need urgently to study how to preserve and protect our present resources. A farsighted national policy to deal with all aspects of our remaining wildlife and natural resources can be the only answer.

One of man's greatest challenges is to reconcile himself with nature, for man in this industrial age dominates his environment so completely that there are few untrammeled areas remaining. If we do nothing, or make only a feeble effort, then our air, water, and other vital resources will continue to further deteriorate. Can the past trend be slowed or stopped? The answer is yes, because it must be yes. Man cannot pretend much longer that he is not an integral part of the all-embracing web of life; for if man alters the environment too much, he, too, may well become a vanishing species.

When the last corner lot is covered with tenements we can still make a playground by tearing them down, but when the last antelope goes by the board, not all the playground associations in Christendom can do aught to replace the loss.

From "Goose Music" by Aldo Leopold

Bison, commonly called "buffalo," once grazed our American plains by the millions. A perfect example of man's past greed, complete extermination was only prevented by heroic efforts by the government. Public outrage saved this monarch of the plains, and today a few small herds once again roam our Western national parks.